# SIMPLY THE BEST
## ANYTIME POWER BLENDING RECIPES

### MARIAN GETZ

Copyright © 2011 Marian Getz

www.cookbookdesigner.com

Printed in the U.S.A.

A most sincere thank you to our wonderful viewers and customers for without you, there would be no need for a cookbook.

Thank you, Wolfgang, for your passionate leadership. To be able to work with you makes me the luckiest person I know. There is no other chef I can think of in the whole world that I would rather work for. I respect you and am incredibly proud to work for you. That you possess such a witty sense of humor is just the icing on the cake.

To my husband Greg, your love is my most cherished recipe of all. Thanks, honey, for finding the ways to encourage me, for nudging me onward and for telling me I can do it even when I don't believe it myself. You are the best part of me. Thanks also for so sweetly sharing the couch with me and my invasive, teetering stacks of cookbooks and magazines. For my sons, Jordan and Ben, daughter-in-law Lindsay and grandson Easton. You make everything in my life so much sweeter. I love you. To Mom and Dad, one of the greatest influences you have had on my life is through the beautiful example of your love for one another.

To our hard working team of cooks behind the scenes at HSN who make magic happen each and every show so that the food being cooked by Wolf on-air comes out beautifully every time.

When you are lucky enough to work for Wolfgang Puck, you are also ever so fortunate to work with the likes of Sydney Silverman, Mike Sanseverino, Arnie Simon, Phoebe Soong, Nicolle Squire, Michael Simon, Debra Murray and many other wonderful people at the office.

Special thanks to our editor and photographer Daniel Koren, for your gentle patience and for giving my garbled words and scribbled recipes a sweet voice and a story. You take such beautiful photographs. You have taken my humble food and captured it on film so that each photo makes me hungry.

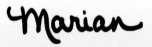

The modern tools we have in the kitchen, whether in the restaurant or at home, are expected to be able to do more than one thing. While a blender is typically thought of as an appliance that can only make shakes or drinks, it is capable of performing a variety of tasks. The blender is a kitchen tool that can be used to make anything from breakfast to dinner and even snacks.

Marian's blender cookbook is a wonderful collection of recipes for this appliance. She has taken her experiences as a chef, mother, and now a grandmother, and created an amazing guide for the user to follow and be successful. Her recipes are easy to follow and they taste incredible as well.

A student of cooking is probably one of the best ways to describe Marian. She is always looking for something new, something fresh, something local, something seasonal. Her culinary knowledge combined with her passion for cooking is second to none. The recipes that Marian has written for this cookbook and the ease of which they can be prepared will motivate you to become more creative in the kitchen.

I know that her philosophy of cooking is the same as mine – use great ingredients and make awesome food!

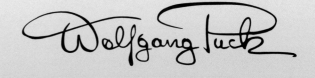

**INTRODUCTION BY WOLFGANG PUCK**

3

TABLE OF CONTENTS

# BLENDER TIPS

## Monitoring The Blender

Watch closely when using your blender. It operates so fast that it can be easy to over mix some recipes so monitor the progress carefully. Only blend ingredients to the desired consistency. If you over blend, the blender can create enough friction that it quickly heats the ingredients you have inside. This is fine when making soups or sauces but it is not desirable if you are making smoothies or ice cream. This blender operates far more quickly than average blenders.

## Stir Stick

The stir stick that comes with your blender will help you push all of the ingredients towards the blade. This is a wonderful thing because it eliminates the need to stop the blender and scrape it down using a spatula. This is an enormous time saver for busy cooks.

## Sauces

For emulsified sauces such as mayonnaise or Hollandaise sauce, pour the oil or melted butter through the filler hole while blending. Pour it in a slow stream to avoid the oil pooling on top of the other ingredients. This will ensure that the sauce comes out smooth and creamy. To prevent spattering when adding ingredients, hold a folded kitchen towel to cover most of the filler hole while adding ingredients. Another trick is to place a short funnel in the filler cap opening.

## Controlling Splashing

When pureeing hot soups or liquids, always start off on LOW and place a folded kitchen towel over the blender lid. This will help control splashing and steam. Increase the speed once the ingredients are pureed. Make sure to fill the blender only ¼ full of any hot liquid and have the filler cap on loosely so that steam does not lift it off while pureeing.

## Protein Shakes

If you are using the blender to make protein shakes I suggest adding all of the other ingredients first, starting with the liquid part, blend until smooth, then add the protein powder and PULSE until mixed. This helps control excess foaminess.

## Dense Ingredients & Mixtures

When using your blender for recipes that include dense ingredients, the motor of your blender may make different types of noises. This is normal as the sounds can change when the blender is working harder.

## Cleaning Your Blender

For cleaning the blender jar, use a small brush similar to those created for cleaning baby bottles. It is a very helpful tool to get the small seeds out from along the gasket area of the blender. For general cleaning, I suggest adding 2 inches of warm water to the blender with a small amount of dish washing detergent. Cover and blend on LOW to let the power of the blender do the cleaning for you.

# PANTRY TIPS

Being prepared to cook the recipes in this book, or any recipe for that matter, is one of the keys to success in the kitchen. Your pantry must be stocked with the basics. We all know how frustrating it can be when you go to the cupboard and what you need is not there. This list includes some of the ingredients you will find in this book and some that we feel are important to always have on hand.

## Perishables:

Onions
Garlic
Tomatoes
Carrots
Celery
Ginger
Bell Peppers
White Potatoes
Sweet Potatoes
Squashes
Citrus
Apples
Bananas
Lettuce
Spinach
Fresh Herbs
Green Onions
Milk
Cream Cheese
Parmesan Cheese
Yogurt
Other Cheeses You Like

## Spices:

Kosher Salt
Pepper
Bay Leaves
Sage
Oregano
Thyme
Chili Flakes
Cumin Seeds
Curry Powder
Onion Powder
Garlic Powder
Dry Mustard
Ground Cinnamon
Nutmeg
Cloves
Chili Powder

## Dry goods:

Sugars
Sugar Substitute
Vanilla
Extracts/Flavorings
Agave Syrup
Canned Tomatoes
Canned Beans
Canned Vegetables
Dried Chilies
Pasta
Lentils
Stocks
Powdered Bouillon
Olives
Ketchup
Mustard
Pickles
Oils
Vinegar
Honey

*It is not necessary to have all the items listed at all times. However, if you are feeling creative, adventurous or just following a recipe, it's great to have a good selection in the kitchen.*

# BLUEBERRY PANCAKES

**Makes 4 servings**

## Ingredients:

**For the Pancakes:**

1 large egg

1 cup all purpose flour

1 cup whole milk

⅓ cup plain Greek yogurt

2 tablespoons granulated sugar

1 tablespoon unsalted butter, melted

2 teaspoons baking powder

½ teaspoon kosher salt

1 cup fresh blueberries

**For the Skillet:**

Unsalted butter, as needed

## Method:

1. *Place all pancake ingredients, except blueberries, into the blender; cover with lid.*
2. *Blend on LOW for 20 seconds or until smooth (use stir stick as needed).*
3. *In a nonstick skillet over medium-high heat, melt some butter and swirl to coat the skillet.*
4. *Pour batter into the skillet, ¼ cup at a time, to make multiple pancakes.*
5. *Top each pancake with 2 tablespoons of blueberries.*
6. *Cook for 2-3 minutes or until bottom is golden brown and bubbles form on the surface.*
7. *Flip pancakes over and cook for 2-3 minutes or until golden brown.*
8. *Repeat with remaining batter.*
9. *Serve as desired.*

# BANANA PANCAKES

**Makes 4 servings**

## Ingredients:

**For the Pancakes:**

2 large eggs

1 cup all purpose flour

1 cup whole milk

2 tablespoons unsalted butter, melted

½ teaspoon baking powder

½ teaspoon kosher salt

2 bananas, thinly sliced

**For the Skillet:**

Unsalted butter, as needed

## Method:

1. Place all pancake ingredients, except bananas, into the blender; cover with lid.
2. Blend on LOW for 20 seconds or until smooth (use stir stick as needed).
3. In a nonstick skillet over medium-high heat, melt some butter and swirl to coat the skillet.
4. Pour batter into the skillet, ¼ cup at a time, to make multiple pancakes.
5. Top each pancake with banana slices.
6. Cook for 2-3 minutes or until bottom is golden brown and bubbles form on the surface.
7. Flip pancakes over and cook for 2-3 minutes or until golden brown.
8. Repeat with remaining batter.
9. Serve as desired.

# BUTTERMILK WAFFLES

**Makes 4 servings**

## Ingredients:

2 large eggs, separated

1½ cups buttermilk

¼ cup unsalted butter, melted and divided

2 tablespoons brown sugar, packed

1½ cups all purpose flour

1 tablespoon baking powder

¼ teaspoon ground cinnamon

½ teaspoon kosher salt

## Method:

1. *Place the egg whites into the blender; cover with lid.*
2. *Blend on HIGH until frothy then pour into a bowl; set aside.*
3. *Place the egg yolks, buttermilk, 3 tablespoons butter and sugar into the blender; cover with lid.*
4. *Blend on LOW until frothy and combined (use stir stick as needed).*
5. *Add the flour, baking powder, cinnamon and salt; cover with lid.*
6. *Blend on LOW until smooth (use stir stick as needed).*
7. *Add the whipped egg whites while PULSING.*
8. *Let batter rest for 20 minutes.*
9. *Preheat a waffle maker and brush with some of the remaining butter.*
10. *Pour the batter into the waffle maker according to manufacturer's instructions.*
11. *Cook for 5-7 minutes or until golden brown.*
12. *Remove waffle and repeat with remaining batter.*
13. *Top as desired and serve.*

# EASY
# CREPES

**Makes about 24 crepes**

## Ingredients:

5 large eggs

3 cups whole milk

2 tablespoons unsalted butter, melted

1 teaspoon kosher salt

1 tablespoon brandy

1 teaspoon vanilla extract

1 tablespoon sugar

2 cups unbleached all purpose flour

## Method:

1. *Place all ingredients in the order listed above into the blender; cover with lid.*
2. *Blend on LOW for 1 minute or until smooth.*
3. *Preheat a small skillet or crepe pan over medium heat.*
4. *Pour a small amount of oil on the hot pan and swirl to coat evenly.*
5. *Add 2 tablespoons of crepe batter to the skillet and swirl to form a crepe.*
6. *If there are holes, add additional batter, if there is excess batter, pour it out.*
7. *Cook for 30 seconds or until the edges look dry.*
8. *Use a small off-set spatula to lift the edge of the crepe.*
9. *Flip over and cook for 10 seconds.*
10. *Invert pan over a plate to release the crepe.*
11. *Add a bit more oil, swirl to coat and repeat with remaining batter.*
12. *Fill and serve as desired.*
13. *Crepes can be covered and frozen for up to 1 month.*

## TIP
Place a piece of parchment paper between each crepe after cooking to prevent sticking.

# BUCKWHEAT CREPES

**Makes about 14 crepes**

## Ingredients:

⅔ cup buckwheat flour

½ cup all purpose flour

2 large eggs

1 cup whole milk

⅔ cup water

2 tablespoons unsalted butter, melted and divided

1 teaspoon kosher salt

## Method:

1. *In a bowl, combine the buckwheat flour and all purpose flour; whisk then set aside.*

2. *Place eggs, milk, water, 1 tablespoon butter and salt into the blender; cover with lid.*

3. *Blend on LOW until thoroughly combined.*

4. *Pour the flour mixture through the filler cap hole and blend on LOW until smooth.*

5. *Brush some of the remaining butter on a crepe pan or skillet over medium-high heat.*

6. *Pour ¼ cup of batter into the pan; quickly swirl to cover the pan's surface.*

7. *Cook for 3 minutes or until golden brown.*

8. *Flip crepe over and cook for an additional 30 seconds.*

9. *Invert pan over a plate to release the crepe.*

10. *Repeat with remaining batter.*

11. *Fill as desired with fruit, jam or whipped cream.*

# DUTCH BABY

**Makes 4 servings**

## Ingredients:

¾ cup whole milk

3 eggs

¾ cup all purpose flour

½ teaspoon kosher salt

4 tablespoons butter

3 cups fresh berries or bananas

Maple syrup

Powdered sugar

## Method:

1. *Place the milk, eggs, flour and salt into the blender; cover with lid.*
2. *Blend on MEDIUM for 1 minute (use stir stick as needed).*
3. *Let batter rest for 20 minutes.*
4. *Preheat the oven to 450°F and place the oven rack in the bottom third of the oven.*
5. *Place a 12-inch sauté pan with sloped sides and oven-proof handle in the oven.*
6. *Heat pan for 10 minutes or until very hot.*
7. *Add the butter to the hot pan; let melt for 4-5 minutes or until very hot.*
8. *Pour the batter into the center of pan.*
9. *Bake for 20-25 minutes or until Dutch Baby is dramatically puffed and brown.*
10. *Using potholders, remove the sauté pan from the oven to a trivet or towel-lined platter.*
11. *Pour the berries into the center of the Dutch Baby.*
12. *Top with syrup and dust with powdered sugar before serving.*

# STUFFED PISTACHIO FRENCH TOAST

**Makes 4 servings**

## Ingredients:

1 loaf brioche or challah bread, hand-sliced into 8 thick slices

1 cup cream cheese, softened

6 large eggs

½ teaspoon pure vanilla extract

2 cups heavy cream

1½ cups pistachio nuts, chopped

Butter

Maple syrup

Powdered sugar

## Method:

1. *Using a small knife, cut a pocket into the side of each bread slice; set aside.*

2. *Place cream cheese into a pastry bag or plastic zipper bag with a corner snipped.*

3. *Use bag to neatly pipe 2 tablespoons of cream cheese into each bread pocket.*

4. *Place eggs, vanilla and cream into the blender; cover with lid.*

5. *Blend on LOW for 30 seconds or until smooth.*

6. *Pour mixture into a shallow bowl large enough to hold the bread slices.*

7. *Spread the pistachio nuts on a plate.*

8. *Heat a large sauté pan over medium heat.*

9. *Dip each bread slice into the egg mixture on both sides then dip one side firmly into the pistachio nuts.*

10. *Apply nonstick spray to the sauté pan.*

11. *Place bread slices nut-side up into the sauté pan, cooking in batches if necessary.*

12. *Cook for 3-4 minutes or until golden brown.*

13. *Flip over and cook for an additional 2 minutes.*

14. *Top with butter, syrup or powdered sugar before serving hot.*

# POTATO & SPINACH FRITTATA

**Makes 2 servings**

## Ingredients:

2 tablespoons canola oil

6 small red potatoes, sliced

1 cup fresh spinach, packed

2 tablespoons green onions, sliced

1 fresh garlic clove, crushed

Kosher salt to taste

Freshly ground pepper to taste

6 large eggs

⅓ cup whole milk

½ cup Cheddar cheese, shredded

## Method:

1. *Heat oil in a medium skillet over medium heat.*
2. *Add potatoes to the skillet; cover.*
3. *Cook for 10 minutes or until tender.*
4. *Mix in the spinach, green onions and garlic.*
5. *Season with salt and pepper then continue to cook for 1-2 minutes or until spinach is wilted.*
6. *Place the eggs and milk into the blender; cover with lid.*
7. *PULSE for 5 seconds or until frothy.*
8. *Pour egg mixture over the vegetables in the skillet.*
9. *Sprinkle with cheese then reduce the heat to low; cover.*
10. *Cook for 5-7 minutes or until eggs are firm.*
11. *Serve immediately.*

# SOUTHERN STYLE OMELET

**Makes 2 servings**

## Ingredients:

6 large eggs

⅔ cup Cheddar cheese, cubed

1 small yellow onion, peeled and quartered

⅓ cup whole milk

2 tablespoons unsalted butter

4 bacon strips, cooked and crumbled

½ cup ham, diced

½ cup pork sausage, cooked and crumbled

½ cup Swiss cheese, shredded

Kosher salt to taste

Freshly ground pepper to taste

## Method:

1. *Preheat your broiler to HIGH.*
2. *Place the eggs, Cheddar cheese, onions and milk into the blender; cover with lid.*
3. *Blend on HIGH for 30 seconds or until foamy.*
4. *Preheat a large oven-safe omelet pan over medium heat.*
5. *Add the butter and swirl to coat the pan.*
6. *Pour the egg mixture into the pan; shake pan gently for 1 minute.*
7. *Use a spatula to push the edges of the omelet towards the center of the pan to allow the liquid egg to flow underneath and cook.*
8. *When half of the liquid egg remains, scatter remaining ingredients over the egg.*
9. *Put the pan under the broiler for 5 minutes or until browned then remove.*
10. *Use a spatula to fold omelet in half and serve.*

# COLD CUCUMBER SOUP

**Makes 4 servings**

## Ingredients:

1 large English cucumber, trimmed, seeded and cut into chunks

2 cups plain Greek yogurt

1 tablespoon fresh lemon juice

2 teaspoons kosher salt

¼ teaspoon granulated sugar

¼ cup cold water

## Method:

1. *Place all ingredients into the blender; cover with lid.*
2. *Blend on LOW for 30 seconds or until smooth (use stir stick as needed).*
3. *Ladle into bowls and serve.*

**TIP**

For a more delicate color
and flavor of soup,
you can peel the cucumber first.

# BUTTERNUT
# SQUASH SOUP

**Makes 6 servings**

## Ingredients:

2 tablespoons unsalted butter

1 tablespoon olive oil

2 cups yellow onions, chopped

2 pounds butternut squash, peeled and cut into chunks

3 cups chicken stock

2 teaspoons kosher salt

½ teaspoon freshly ground black pepper

1 tablespoon honey

2 teaspoons apple cider vinegar

1 cup half & half

## Method:

1. *Place the butter and oil into an 8-quart stockpot over medium heat.*
2. *When hot, add the onions and cook for 5 minutes or until translucent.*
3. *Add the squash, stock, salt, pepper, honey and vinegar; cover.*
4. *Reduce heat to medium-low and simmer for 30 minutes or until squash is fork tender.*
5. *Pour ⅓ of the squash mixture into the blender; cover with lid.*
6. *Blend on LOW first to avoid splashing then increase speed to HIGH and blend until smooth.*
7. *Pour into a serving tureen and repeat with remaining soup.*
8. *Add half & half to the soup and stir until combined.*
9. *Ladle into bowls and serve.*

**TIP**

You will notice that most of my savory recipes contain something salty, sweet, tart and spicy. Taste before serving a dish to determine if it needs additional seasoning. Most of the time, you may need to add something salty, sweet, tart or spicy. Once I figured out this flavor balance, my food got a whole lot better.

# SWEET CORN
## SOUP

**Makes 4 servings**

## Ingredients:

1 small yellow onion, quartered

2 tablespoons unsalted butter

1 teaspoon kosher salt

4 cups chicken stock

$\frac{2}{3}$ cup half & half

1 medium Russet potato, peeled and quartered

2 cups frozen yellow corn kernels, thawed

1 teaspoon fresh lemon juice

## Method:

1. *Place all ingredients into the blender; cover with lid.*
2. *Blend on LOW for 30 seconds (use stir stick as needed).*
3. *Blend on HIGH for 4 minutes or until very steamy and hot.*
4. *Carefully remove the lid and adjust seasoning if desired.*
5. *Ladle into bowls and serve hot.*

# CARROT
# SOUP

**Makes 4 servings**

## Ingredients:

2 tablespoons unsalted butter

4 cups carrots, peeled and sliced

2 green onions, chopped

¼ teaspoon freshly ground black pepper

2 field cucumbers, peeled, seeded and chopped

⅓ cup long-grain white rice, uncooked

1½ cups water

1 teaspoon kosher salt

2 cups chicken stock, divided

⅓ cup heavy cream

## Method:

1. *Melt the butter in a large saucepan over medium-low heat.*
2. *Add the carrots, green onions and pepper to the saucepan.*
3. *Cook for 10 minutes, stirring occasionally, or until carrots are tender but not browned.*
4. *Stir in the cucumbers, rice, water and salt.*
5. *Increase the temperature to medium-high and bring to a boil.*
6. *Cover and reduce heat to low then simmer for 40 minutes or until rice is very soft.*
7. *Transfer the rice mixture to the blender.*
8. *Add 1 cup chicken stock to the blender; cover with lid.*
9. *Blend on HIGH until smooth.*
10. *Transfer the mixture back to the saucepan and stir in the remaining stock.*
11. *Bring to a boil over medium-high heat then reduce the heat to low and cook for 5 minutes.*
12. *Stir in the heavy cream and cook for an additional 5 minutes.*
13. *Serve in bowls and garnish as desired.*

# CAULIFLOWER & CHEESE SOUP

**Makes 4 servings**

## Ingredients:

8 cups water

1 tablespoon kosher salt

1 head cauliflower, coarsely chopped

1 white onion, quartered

⅔ cup sharp Cheddar cheese, cubed

2 tablespoons unsalted butter

¼ cup heavy cream

⅛ teaspoon cayenne pepper

⅛ teaspoon freshly ground black pepper

2½ cups chicken stock

2 tablespoons chives, finely chopped

## Method:

1. *In a large saucepan over medium-high heat, bring the water and salt to a boil.*

2. *Add the cauliflower and onions; cook for 10 minutes or until tender.*

3. *Drain, reserving ½ cup of the cooking water.*

4. *Transfer half of the cauliflower and onions to the blender.*

5. *Add the cheese, butter, heavy cream, cayenne pepper and black pepper; cover with lid.*

6. *Blend on HIGH for 20 seconds or until smooth (use stir stick as needed).*

7. *Pour mixture back into the saucepan.*

8. *Place remaining cauliflower and onions into the blender.*

9. *Add the reserved cooking liquid to the blender; cover with lid.*

10. *Blend on HIGH for 20 seconds or until smooth (use stir stick as needed).*

11. *Pour mixture back into the saucepan.*

12. *Add the stock and bring to a boil over medium-high heat.*

13. *Reduce heat to low and simmer for 2 minutes.*

14. *Serve topped with chives.*

# EASY
# BORSCHT

**Makes 4 servings**

## Ingredients:

4½ cups water

½ cup dry white wine

1 small onion, chopped

2 teaspoons kosher salt

1½ pounds beets, peeled and quartered

½ cup sour cream

2 sprigs fresh dill

## Method:

1. *Pour the water, wine, onions and salt into a large saucepan over medium-high heat; bring to a boil.*
2. *Add the beets and cook for 45 minutes or until tender.*
3. *Transfer saucepan contents to the blender in batches; cover with lid.*
4. *Blend on HIGH until desired consistency is achieved (use stir stick as needed).*
5. *Transfer blender contents to a large bowl and repeat with remaining saucepan contents.*
6. *Cover bowl with plastic wrap and refrigerate for a minimum of 2 hours.*
7. *For serving, ladle into soup bowls and garnish with sour cream and dill.*

**TIP**

If you prefer to serve hot, place Borscht in saucepan until warm or heat in the microwave.

# PEA SOUP

**Makes 4 servings**

## Ingredients:

3 cups frozen peas, thawed

2 cups lettuce leaves, coarsely chopped

4 green onions

1 tablespoon kosher salt

2½ cups chicken stock

¼ teaspoon granulated sugar

2 tablespoons heavy cream

Croutons

## Method:

1. *Place all ingredients, except croutons, into the blender; cover with lid.*
2. *Blend on HIGH for 6 minutes or until steamy and hot.*
3. *Serve in soup bowls topped with croutons.*

**TIP**

Top this soup with a dollop of sour cream for added flavor.

# CREAMY BROCCOLI
# CHEESE SOUP

**Makes 4-6 servings**

## Ingredients:

1 tablespoon olive oil

1 medium yellow onion, roughly chopped

2 garlic cloves

1 bunch of broccoli, trimmed and chopped

1 Russet potato, diced

3 cups water

1 tablespoon chicken bouillon powder

A few dashes hot sauce

Freshly cracked pepper to taste

1 teaspoon soy sauce

1 tablespoon lemon juice

1 teaspoon honey

¼ cup half & half

⅓ cup Parmesan cheese, grated

## Method:

1. *Place all ingredients into the blender; cover with lid.*
2. *Blend on LOW for 1 minute (use stir stick as needed).*
3. *Blend on HIGH for 4 minutes or until steamy and hot.*
4. *Taste and adjust seasoning if desired.*
5. *Garnish as desired and serve immediately.*

# CREAMY BROCCOLI
# CHEESE SOUP

**Makes 4-6 servings**

## Ingredients:

1 tablespoon olive oil

1 medium yellow onion, roughly chopped

2 garlic cloves

1 bunch of broccoli, trimmed and chopped

1 Russet potato, diced

3 cups water

1 tablespoon chicken bouillon powder

A few dashes hot sauce

Freshly cracked pepper to taste

1 teaspoon soy sauce

1 tablespoon lemon juice

1 teaspoon honey

¼ cup half & half

⅓ cup Parmesan cheese, grated

## Method:

1. *Place all ingredients into the blender; cover with lid.*

2. *Blend on LOW for 1 minute (use stir stick as needed).*

3. *Blend on HIGH for 4 minutes or until steamy and hot.*

4. *Taste and adjust seasoning if desired.*

5. *Garnish as desired and serve immediately.*

# GARLIC SOUP

**Makes 6 servings**

## Ingredients:

3 tablespoons extra virgin olive oil

16 fresh garlic cloves

6 cups boiling water

2 teaspoons kosher salt

12 thin white bread slices

1 teaspoon paprika

## Method:

1. *Pour oil into a large saucepan over medium heat.*
2. *Add garlic and cook for 5 minutes, stirring often, or until garlic is golden brown.*
3. *Add water and salt; cover then reduce heat to low.*
4. *Let simmer for 30 minutes.*
5. *Remove garlic mixture to a bowl and transfer to the blender in batches.*
6. *Blend on HIGH for 30 seconds or until pureed (use stir stick as needed).*
7. *Return blender contents to the saucepan and repeat with remaining garlic mixture.*
8. *Bring saucepan contents to a boil.*
9. *Line up 6 bowls and place 2 bread slices in each bowl.*
10. *Ladle soup over bread and garnish with paprika.*
11. *Serve immediately.*

# FRUIT BASED
# BABY FOOD

**Makes about ¾ cup**

## Ingredients:

**Peaches:**

1 cup fresh peaches

¼ cup water

**Apples:**

1 medium Golden Delicious apple, peeled and cored

¼ cup water

*(Cut apple into quarters and steam until tender)*

**Blueberries:**

1 cup fresh blueberries

¼ cup water

**Plum:**

4 plums, pits removed

¼ cup water

*(Steam plums until soft)*

## Method:

1. *Place desired fruits and water into the blender; cover with lid.*
2. *Blend on HIGH until smooth (use stir stick as needed).*
3. *Put mixture through a fine mesh strainer for a smoother consistency if desired.*
4. *Serve within 2 days or freeze in individual portions for later use.*

**TIP**

The easiest way to freeze individual portions of baby food is in the newer silicone ice cube trays. Just fill to the tops with your baby food, cover and freeze. Once frozen, pop them out into a plastic zipper bag and store. The silicone makes for much easier removal since you can just turn it inside out.

# VEGETABLE BASED
# BABY FOOD
**Makes about ¾ cup**

SOUPS & MORE

## Ingredients:

### Peas
1 cup frozen peas, thawed
⅓ cup water

### Carrots
3 medium carrots, trimmed and peeled
½ cup water
*(Cut carrots into 1-inch pieces and steam until tender)*

### Beets
3 medium fresh beets
¼ cup water
*(Cut beets into 1-inch chunks and steam until tender)*

### Potatoes
2 medium potatoes, peeled
⅔ cup water
*(Cut potatoes into 1-inch chunks and steam until tender)*

## Method:
1. *Place desired vegetables and water into the blender; cover with lid.*
2. *Blend on HIGH until smooth (use stir stick as needed).*
3. *Put mixture through a fine mesh strainer for a smoother consistency if desired.*
4. *Serve immediately or freeze in individual portions for later use.*

## TIP
My favorite way to steam vegetables is using the steamer basket of my rice cooker. Pour about 2 inches of water into the rice cooker, fit the rice cooker with the steamer basket then add the food to the basket. Start checking for doneness after 5 minutes of steaming.

# WHITE BEAN

## DIP

**Makes 2 cups**

## Ingredients:

1 can (15.5 ounces) cannellini beans, drained
2 garlic cloves
1 teaspoon fresh lime zest
Juice of 1 lime
1 teaspoon Adobo all purpose seasoning
1 green onion, chopped
1 teaspoon soy sauce
2 tablespoons canned chipotles en adobo
1 teaspoon honey
2 tablespoons tomato paste
2 tablespoons vegetable oil
Fresh vegetables such as zucchini, carrots, etc.

## Method:

1. *Place all ingredients, except fresh vegetables, into the blender; cover with lid.*
2. *Blend on MEDIUM until smooth (the motor of your blender may make different types of noises as the blender is working harder).*
3. *Use stir stick as needed then blend on HIGH for an additional 30 seconds.*
4. *Taste and correct seasoning if desired.*
5. *Serve with fresh vegetables for dipping.*
6. *Dip can be refrigerated for up to 1 week.*

# CHOCOLATE CHEESECAKE DIP

**Makes about 1½ cups**

## Ingredients:

3 ounces bittersweet chocolate, melted

⅓ cup half & half

2 tablespoons granulated sugar

½ teaspoon vanilla extract

1 package (8 ounces) cream cheese, softened and cut into cubes

## Method:

1. *Place all ingredients, except cream cheese, into the blender; cover with lid.*
2. *Blend on HIGH for 10 seconds.*
3. *While blending, drop the cream cheese cubes, one at a time, through the filler cap hole; blend until smooth (use stir stick as needed).*
4. *Serve immediately.*

**TIP**
You can add a teaspoon of espresso powder to deepen the chocolate flavor.

# BLENDER
# COLESLAW

**Makes 8 servings**

## Ingredients:

### For the Vegetable Mixture:
2 carrots, peeled and roughly cut
1 small head green cabbage, roughly chopped
1 Pink Lady apple, cored and roughly cut
½ red onion, peeled and roughly cut
Water

### For the Mayonnaise Mixture:
1 cup mayonnaise
⅓ cup buttermilk
2 tablespoons apple cider vinegar
2 teaspoons granulated sugar
1 teaspoon yellow mustard
½ teaspoon kosher salt
¼ teaspoon freshly ground black pepper

## Method:

1. Place carrots, cabbage, apples and onions into the blender until half full.
2. Add enough water until it reaches 2 inches from the top; cover with lid.
3. Blend on LOW for 10 seconds or until finely chopped.
4. Transfer mixture to a fine mesh strainer.
5. Repeat until all vegetables are chopped.
6. Squeeze as much water from the vegetables as possible.
7. Transfer vegetables to a large bowl.
8. Rinse the blender then place all mayonnaise mixture ingredients into the blender; cover with lid.
9. Blend on LOW for 15 seconds or until mixed well (use stir stick as needed).
10. Pour the mayonnaise mixture over the vegetables; mix well.
11. Cover and refrigerate for a minimum of 1 hour before serving.
12. Coleslaw will keep in the refrigerator for up to 3 days.

# HOMEMADE
# PEANUT BUTTER

**Makes ¾ cup**

## Ingredients:

2 cups roasted peanuts

## Method:

1. *Place the peanuts into the blender; cover with lid.*
2. *Blend on LOW until chopped (use stir stick as needed).*
3. *Increase speed to HIGH and blend for 2-3 minutes or until nuts turn into a fairly smooth peanut butter (the motor of your blender may make different types of noises as the blender is working harder).*
4. *Remove to a covered jar or container.*
5. *Store peanut butter airtight at room temperature and use within 1 week.*
6. *Natural oil from the peanuts will rise to the top over time. I suggest stirring the oil back into the peanut butter rather than pouring it off to avoid it becoming stiff and dry in texture.*

## TIP

Sometimes I add a handful of chocolate chips and make a delicious chocolate flavored nut butter that tastes best eaten right out of the jar using a spoon.

# ORANGE CRANBERRY
# RELISH

**Makes 2 cups**

## Ingredients:

1 large orange, ends trimmed and quartered

3 cups fresh or frozen cranberries

1 celery stalk

1 cup granulated sugar, or to taste

½ cup pecans or walnuts, toasted

## Method:

1. *Place all ingredients into the blender; cover with lid.*
2. *Blend on LOW until pieces are small but still chunky (use stir stick as needed).*
3. *Remove to a covered jar or container.*
4. *Refrigerate for a minimum of 2 hours before serving.*

**TIP**

For a change of flavor, add
a cup of chopped fresh or frozen
rhubarb before blending.

# CURRY
# MAYONNAISE

**Makes about 2 cups**

## Ingredients:

2 garlic cloves

2 cups mayonnaise, store-bought or see recipe on page 50

2 tablespoons fresh lemon juice

2 teaspoons honey

2 teaspoons curry powder

½ teaspoon ground ginger

¼ teaspoon ground cumin

¼ teaspoon ground cloves

¼ teaspoon fresh black pepper

2 teaspoons fresh or dry turmeric

## Method:

1. *Place all ingredients into the blender; cover with lid.*
2. *Blend on LOW until garlic is minced (use stir stick as needed).*
3. *Transfer to an airtight container.*
4. *Mayonnaise will keep in the refrigerator for up to 1 week.*

**TIP**
For bright yellow
curry mayo, use
fresh turmeric.

Curry Mayo

# HOMEMADE
# MAYONNAISE

**Makes 2 cups**

## Ingredients:

2 large eggs
1 teaspoon fine sea salt
1 tablespoon dry mustard
1 tablespoon white vinegar
1 tablespoon fresh lemon juice
A pinch of white pepper (optional)
2 cups canola oil

## Method:

1. *Place all ingredients, except oil, into the blender; cover with lid.*
2. *Blend on HIGH for 30 seconds.*
3. *While blending, pour oil in a slow stream through the filler cap hole, not letting the oil pool on top of the mayonnaise.*
4. *Blend until thickened.*
5. *Transfer to an airtight container.*
6. *Mayonnaise will keep in the refrigerator for up to 1 week.*

**TIP**
You can use pasteurized eggs if you want to avoid consuming raw eggs.

# HORSERADISH
# MUSTARD

**Makes about 1 ⅓ cups**

## Ingredients:

½ cup dry mustard

¼ cup mustard seeds

½ cup cider vinegar

¼ cup warm water

2 tablespoons horseradish

2 teaspoons kosher salt

## Method:

1. *Place all ingredients into the blender; cover with lid.*
2. *Blend on HIGH for 30 seconds or until smooth with some seeds remaining (use stir stick as needed).*
3. *Transfer to an airtight container.*
4. *Mustard will keep in the refrigerator for up to 3 months.*

**TIP**
This mustard is best served with baked ham.

# CAULIFLOWER PUREE

**Makes 4 servings**

## Ingredients:

1 large head of cauliflower, cut into florets

1 cup chicken stock

½ cup whole milk or half & half

Kosher salt to taste

Freshly cracked pepper to taste

3 tablespoons unsalted butter

Green Onions, sliced

## Method:

1. *Place all ingredients, except butter and green onions, into a large saucepan over medium heat; cover with a tight fitting lid.*

2. *Bring to a boil then reduce heat to a simmer.*

3. *Cook for 15 minutes or until cauliflower is fork tender; remove from heat.*

4. *Drain and reserve most of the liquid.*

5. *Place drained cauliflower into the blender; cover with lid.*

6. *Blend on LOW first to avoid splashing then increase speed to HIGH and blend until very smooth (use stir stick as needed).*

7. *Blend in the butter and enough reserved liquid to achieve a soft texture.*

8. *Taste carefully and adjust seasoning if desired.*

9. *Serve topped with green onions.*

# MEXICAN GREEN RICE

**Makes 6 servings**

## Ingredients:

1 cup fresh spinach leaves, packed

½ bunch fresh cilantro, packed

1 teaspoon kosher salt

1½ cups chicken stock

1 tablespoon unsalted butter

1 tablespoon vegetable oil

2 garlic cloves, minced

1 medium white onion, finely chopped

2 cups long-grain white rice, uncooked

1 cup whole milk

## Method:

1. *Place the spinach, cilantro, salt and stock into the blender; cover with lid.*
2. *Blend on HIGH for 20 seconds or until pureed (use stir stick as needed).*
3. *Set spinach mixture aside.*
4. *Heat the butter and oil in a large saucepan over medium heat.*
5. *Add the garlic and onions; cook for 6 minutes or until onions are soft.*
6. *Stir in the rice and cook until oil is absorbed, stirring constantly.*
7. *Pour in the spinach mixture and bring to a boil.*
8. *Cover and reduce heat to low; simmer for 10 minutes or until liquid is absorbed.*
9. *Stir in the milk and cook for an additional 10 minutes or until the rice is tender.*
10. *Remove from heat and let stand for 10 minutes before serving.*

# OLD FASHIONED
# SPOON BREAD

**Makes 4-6 servings**

## Ingredients:

5 large eggs

1¾ cups whole milk

2 tablespoons yellow mustard

1 tablespoon kosher salt

½ teaspoon freshly ground pepper

⅔ cup all purpose flour

½ cup mozzarella cheese, shredded

1 cup Parmesan cheese, grated

½ cup unsalted butter, melted

1 cup yellow cornmeal

1 teaspoon hot sauce

2 cups frozen yellow corn, thawed

1 large yellow onion, chopped

¼ cup flat leaf parsley, chopped

## Method:

1. *Preheat oven to 375°F and butter a 9x13-inch baking pan; set aside.*
2. *Place eggs into the blender; cover with lid then blend on HIGH for 1 minute.*
3. *Add the milk, mustard, salt, pepper, flour, cheeses, butter, cornmeal and hot sauce; cover with lid.*
4. *Blend on MEDIUM for 30 seconds (use stir stick as needed).*
5. *Add remaining ingredients; cover with lid then blend on MEDIUM for 3 seconds.*
6. *Pour mixture into the prepared pan and bake for 40-50 minutes.*
7. *Spoon bread is done when slightly puffed and well browned.*
8. *Remove and serve warm.*

# HOLLANDAISE
# SAUCE

**Makes 2 cups**

## Ingredients:

6 egg yolks

⅓ cup fresh lemon juice

1 teaspoon kosher salt

¼ teaspoon cayenne pepper

¼ teaspoon freshly ground white pepper

1 cup unsalted butter, melted

## Method:

1. *Place all ingredients, except butter, into the blender; cover with lid.*
2. *Blend on HIGH for 10 seconds or until smooth.*
3. *While blending, pour the butter in a thin stream through the filler cap hole until incorporated.*
4. *Keep warm in a bowl over hot (not boiling) water until ready to serve.*

# HOLLANDAISE
## SAUCE

**Makes 2 cups**

## Ingredients:

6 egg yolks

⅓ cup fresh lemon juice

1 teaspoon kosher salt

¼ teaspoon cayenne pepper

¼ teaspoon freshly ground white pepper

1 cup unsalted butter, melted

## Method:

# HOMEMADE
# PIZZA SAUCE

**Makes 3 cups**

## Ingredients:

1 can (28 ounces) whole stewed tomatoes

¼ cup tomato paste

2 teaspoons granulated sugar

1 small handful fresh basil

2 teaspoons fresh oregano

4 garlic cloves, minced

½ teaspoon kosher salt

¼ teaspoon freshly ground pepper

## Method:

1. *Place all ingredients into the blender; cover with lid.*
2. *Blend on HIGH for 30 seconds or until smooth (use stir stick as needed).*
3. *Pour into 3 freezer-safe containers and cover.*
4. *Pizza sauce will keep in the freezer for up to 3 months.*

## TIP
Even though this sauce can be used immediately, it is better when frozen for 2 weeks, thawed and then used.

# ASIAN STYLE PEANUT
# DRESSING

**Makes about 1 cup**

## Ingredients:

1 Thai bird chili pepper, or to taste

2 garlic cloves

½ cup crunchy peanut butter

Zest and juice of 1 lime

1 tablespoon granulated sugar

1 teaspoon fish sauce

¼ cup coconut milk

## Method:

1. *Place all ingredients into the blender; cover with lid.*
2. *Blend on HIGH until desired consistency.*
3. *Pour dressing into a container.*
4. *Dressing will keep in the refrigerator for up to 3 days.*
5. *Bring to room temperature before serving.*

## TIP
This dressing is delicious stirred into hot spaghetti or soba noodles for a quick meal.

# CAESAR SALAD
# DRESSING

**Makes about 2 cups**

## Ingredients:

4 anchovy fillets

3 garlic cloves

2 large eggs

¼ cup fresh lemon juice

2 tablespoons red wine vinegar

½ teaspoon freshly ground black pepper

½ teaspoon kosher salt

½ teaspoon Worcestershire sauce

½ teaspoon hot pepper sauce

1¼ cups extra virgin olive oil

1 cup Parmesan cheese, grated

## Method:

1. *Place all ingredients, except olive oil and cheese, into the blender; cover with lid.*
2. *Blend on HIGH for 30 seconds or until smooth and creamy.*
3. *While blending, pour oil in a slow stream through the filler cap hole, not letting the oil pool on top of the dressing; blend until smooth.*
4. *Add the cheese and blend on HIGH until combined.*
5. *Pour dressing into a container.*
6. *Dressing will keep in the refrigerator for up to 3 days.*

# CREAMY CILANTRO DRESSING

**Makes about 2 cups**

## Ingredients:

⅓ cup cream of coconut

½ teaspoon sriracha chili sauce

2 teaspoons dry mustard

1 bunch cilantro, stems trimmed

1 bunch mint leaves

1 tablespoon fresh ginger

1 large egg, pasteurized (optional)

Zest and juice of 2 limes

1 tablespoon soy sauce

4 garlic cloves

⅓ cup rice wine vinegar

1 teaspoon kosher salt

1 tablespoon toasted sesame oil

1½ cups peanut oil

## Method:

1. *Place all ingredients, except peanut oil, into the blender; cover with lid.*
2. *Blend on LOW for 5 seconds (use stir stick as needed).*
3. *Increase speed to HIGH.*
4. *While blending, pour oil in a slow stream through the filler cap hole, not letting the oil pool on top of the dressing.*
5. *Blend for 30 seconds (use stir stick as needed).*
6. *Taste and adjust seasoning if desired.*
7. *Pour dressing into a container.*
8. *Dressing can be stored airtight in the refrigerator for up to 1 week.*

# CUCUMBER DRESSING

**Makes about 1¼ cups**

## Ingredients:

⅔ cup plain yogurt

2 tablespoons lemon juice, freshly squeezed

½ teaspoon kosher salt

¼ teaspoon fresh black pepper

¼ teaspoon granulated sugar

Pinch of cayenne pepper

½ English cucumber, seeded and cut into chunks

2 tablespoons cilantro

1 green onion

## Method:

1. *Place all ingredients, except cilantro and green onion, into the blender; cover with lid.*
2. *Blend on HIGH for 15 seconds.*
3. *Add the cilantro and green onion; cover with lid.*
4. *PULSE until combined.*
5. *Pour dressing into a container.*
6. *Dressing will keep in the refrigerator for 3 days.*

# MY FAVORITE CURRY DRESSING

**Makes 2 cups**

## Ingredients:

1 tablespoon curry powder

⅛ teaspoon ground cardamom

½ teaspoon turmeric powder

2 tablespoons fresh ginger, peeled

4 garlic cloves

1 green onion

1 handful cilantro leaves

1 handful mint leaves

¼ cup apple cider vinegar

½ teaspoon sriracha or hot sauce

1 teaspoon soy sauce

½ cup canned cream of coconut

1 tablespoon kosher salt

1 large egg, pasteurized (optional)

1½ cups canola oil

## Method:

1. *Place all ingredients, except oil, into the blender; cover with lid.*
2. *Blend on MEDIUM for 20 seconds (use stir stick as needed).*
3. *Increase speed to HIGH.*
4. *While blending, pour oil in a slow stream through the filler cap hole, not letting the oil pool on top of the dressing.*
5. *Blend on MEDIUM for 1 minute or until thick and smooth.*
6. *Pour dressing into a container.*
7. *Dressing will keep in the refrigerator for up to 1 week.*

# AVOCADO
# DRESSING

**Makes about 1½ cups**

## Ingredients:

1 avocado, peeled and pit removed

1 garlic clove

½ cup plain yogurt

2 tablespoons canola oil

2 tablespoons fresh lemon juice

1 tablespoon white wine vinegar

1 teaspoon kosher salt, or to taste

¼ teaspoon freshly ground black pepper

Pinch of ground cumin

Pinch of chili flakes

## Method:

1. *Place all ingredients into the blender; cover with lid.*
2. *Blend on HIGH for 15 seconds.*
3. *Pour dressing into a container.*
4. *Dressing will keep in the refrigerator for up to 3 days.*

# GREEN GODDESS
# DRESSING

**Makes about 1-2 cups**

## Ingredients:

1 garlic clove

1 packed cup of a mixture of tarragon leaves, parsley, basil leaves and spinach leaves

1 large egg

¼ cup apple cider vinegar

1 anchovy fillet (about 1 teaspoon)

1 teaspoon capers

1 tablespoon granulated sugar

2 teaspoons kosher salt

¼ teaspoon fresh cracked pepper

1 cup canola oil

## Method:

1. *Place all ingredients, except oil, into the blender; cover with lid.*
2. *Blend on LOW until fairly smooth (use stir stick as needed).*
3. *Increase speed to HIGH.*
4. *While blending, pour oil in a slow stream through the filler cap hole, not letting the oil pool on top of the dressing.*
5. *Blend for an additional 30 seconds (use stir stick as needed).*
6. *Taste and adjust seasoning, adding more sugar and salt if desired.*
7. *Pour dressing into a container.*
8. *Dressing will keep in the refrigerator for up to 3 days.*

# POPPY SEED DRESSING

**Makes 2 cups**

## Ingredients:

1 garlic clove
¼ medium yellow onion, peeled
⅓ cup honey
¼ cup fresh lemon juice
2 tablespoons apple cider vinegar
2 teaspoons Dijon mustard
1 teaspoon kosher salt, or to taste
¼ teaspoon chili flakes
2 tablespoons poppy seeds
1 cup canola oil

## Method:

1. *Place all ingredients, except poppy seeds and oil, into the blender; cover with lid.*
2. *Blend on HIGH for 15 seconds or until onions and garlic are finely chopped.*
3. *Add poppy seeds to the blender; cover with lid.*
4. *Decrease speed to LOW.*
5. *While blending, pour oil in a slow stream through the filler cap hole, not letting the oil pool on top of the dressing; blend until smooth.*
6. *Pour dressing into a container.*
7. *Dressing will keep in the refrigerator for up to 1 week.*

# RASPBERRY
# DRESSING

**Makes 1 cup**

## Ingredients:

2 garlic cloves

⅓ cup raspberries, fresh or frozen

¼ cup canola oil

¼ cup raspberry-flavored vinegar

2 tablespoons sesame oil

2 tablespoons balsamic vinegar

2 teaspoons Dijon mustard

½ teaspoon kosher salt, or to taste

¼ teaspoon freshly ground pepper

## Method:

1. *Place all ingredients into the blender; cover with lid.*
2. *Blend on HIGH for 15 seconds or until smooth.*
3. *Pour dressing into a container.*
4. *Dressing will keep in the refrigerator for up to 1 week.*

# SUGAR FREE MUSTARD
# VINAIGRETTE

**Makes 2 cups**

## Ingredients:

⅓ cup yellow mustard

¼ cup Zsweet sugar substitute or ½ teaspoon stevia

4 tablespoons unflavored fiber powder such as Benefiber

1 garlic clove

¼ small yellow onion

½ cup apple cider vinegar

2 teaspoons kosher salt

2 teaspoons dry mustard

1 anchovy fillet

1 teaspoon Adobo con pimiento

¾ cup avocado or canola oil

½ cup water

## Method:

1. *Place the mustard, sugar substitute, fiber powder, garlic, onion, vinegar, salt, dry mustard, anchovy and Adobo seasoning into the blender; cover with lid.*

2. *Blend on LOW until combined (use stir stick as needed).*

3. *Increase speed to HIGH.*

4. *Pour oil then water in a slow stream through the filler cap hole, not letting the liquid pool on top of the vinaigrette.*

5. *Blend on HIGH for 1 minute.*

6. *Pour vinaigrette into a container.*

7. *Vinaigrette will keep in the refrigerator for up to 1 week.*

# TANGERINE VINAIGRETTE

**Makes 2 cups**

## Ingredients:

2 bright skinned tangerines, halved and seeded but unpeeled

1 green onion, white part only

¼ cup white vinegar

⅓ cup granulated sugar or other sweetener

1 tablespoon kosher salt

1½ cups canola oil

## Method:

1. *Place all ingredients, except oil, into the blender; cover with lid.*
2. *Blend on LOW for 1 minute or until smooth (use stir stick as needed).*
3. *Increase speed to HIGH.*
4. *While blending, pour oil in a slow stream through the filler cap hole, not letting the oil pool on top of the vinaigrette.*
5. *Blend for an additional 30 seconds or until uniform in color and texture.*
6. *Pour vinaigrette into a container.*
7. *Vinaigrette will keep in the refrigerator for up to 1 week.*

**TIP**

You can substitute other citrus fruits for the tangerines. If you choose lime or grapefruit, either use all of it the first day or strain out the pulp before storing as those two fruits have a peel that tends to get bitter.

# EASY PESTO

**Makes 2 cups**

## Ingredients:

4 garlic cloves

4 cups fresh basil leaves, loosely packed

1 cup extra virgin olive oil

¼ cup pine nuts, lightly toasted

2 teaspoons kosher salt

1 cup Parmesan cheese, grated

## Method:

1. *Place all ingredients, except cheese, into the blender; cover with lid.*
2. *Blend on HIGH for 30 seconds or until combined (use stir stick as needed).*
3. *Add the cheese to the blender; cover with lid.*
4. *PULSE to combine.*
5. *Transfer pesto to a container.*
6. *Pesto will keep in the refrigerator for up to 3 days.*

**SAUCES, DRESSINGS & MORE**

**TIP**

For an easy flavor-packed meal, stir some pesto into hot pasta and top with Parmesan cheese.

# CHICKEN
## BOLOGNESE
**Makes 6 servings**

## Ingredients:

1 large yellow onion, quartered

1 large carrot, chunked

1 celery stalk, chunked

1 tablespoon unsalted butter

3 tablespoons tomato paste

½ cup water

1 tablespoon olive oil

1 pound ground chicken

Kosher salt and fresh pepper to taste

2 garlic cloves, chopped

¼ cup dry white wine

3 cups chicken stock

1 can (28 ounces) diced tomatoes

½ cup whole milk

2 tablespoons heavy cream

1 pound pasta, cooked

1 cup ricotta cheese

## Method:

1. *Place the onions, carrots and celery into the blender; cover with lid.*

2. *PULSE until fine.*

3. *Melt the butter in a large saucepan over medium heat.*

4. *Add the onion mixture and sauté for 15 minutes, stirring often, until browned.*

5. *Add tomato paste and cook for an additional 5 minutes to brown the tomato paste.*

6. *Add the water and stir to scrape up all the brown bits from the bottom of the pan.*

7. *Add the olive oil and chicken, then season with salt and pepper.*

8. *Cook for 10 minutes then add the garlic and stir until fragrant.*

9. *Add the wine, stock, tomatoes and milk; stir then season to taste with salt and pepper.*

10. *Cover then reduce heat to low and simmer for 2 hours, stirring occasionally.*

11. *Stir in the cream then taste and adjust seasoning if desired.*

12. *Serve over pasta with a dollop of the ricotta cheese.*

# CHEESE
# SOUFFLÉS

**Makes 4 servings**

## Ingredients:

⅓ cup Parmesan cheese, grated and divided

4 large eggs

1 cup Gruyere cheese, shredded

½ cup cream cheese, softened

⅓ whole milk

½ teaspoon dry mustard

¼ teaspoon kosher salt

⅛ teaspoon freshly ground pepper

2 tablespoons fresh parsley, minced

1 tablespoon fresh chives, minced

## Method:

1. *Preheat oven to 400°F.*
2. *Sprinkle the bottom and sides of four soufflé dishes with 2 tablespoons of Parmesan cheese.*
3. *Place soufflé dishes on a baking sheet.*
4. *Place remaining ingredients, except parsley and chives, into the blender; cover with lid.*
5. *Blend on HIGH for 30 seconds (use stir stick as needed).*
6. *Add the parsley and chives while PULSING.*
7. *Pour mixture into the prepared soufflé dishes.*
8. *Place on the center rack of the oven and bake for 30 minutes or until set.*
9. *Remove and serve immediately.*

**TIP**

These are the easiest soufflés
I know of. No beating or
separating of the eggs first.

# COCONUT SHRIMP

**Makes 4 servings**

## Ingredients:

### For the Shrimp:

Oil for frying

1 cup whole milk

3 large eggs

¼ cup cream of coconut

1¼ cups all purpose flour

1 teaspoon baking powder

2 teaspoons kosher salt

1½ cups shredded coconut

1½ pounds raw shrimp, tail on, peeled and deveined

### For the Dipping Sauce:

⅓ cup Asian sweet chili sauce

⅓ cup cream of coconut

1 green onion, thinly sliced

## Method:

1. *Pour oil into a deep fryer and preheat to 375°F following manufacturer's instructions.*
2. *Place milk, eggs, cream of coconut, flour, baking powder and salt into the blender; cover with lid.*
3. *Blend on LOW for 30 seconds or until very smooth.*
4. *Transfer the batter to a bowl.*
5. *Pour the shredded coconut into a separate bowl.*
6. *Hold a shrimp by the tail and dip into the batter.*
7. *Shake off excess batter then roll the shrimp in shredded coconut until coated.*
8. *Carefully place the shrimp into the fryer and repeat with 5 additional shrimp.*
9. *Fry shrimp for 3-4 minutes or until golden brown.*
10. *Remove and drain on absorbent paper.*
11. *Repeat with remaining shrimp.*
12. *To make the dipping sauce, stir together all sauce ingredients in a bowl.*
13. *Serve hot shrimp with dipping sauce on the side.*

# CHEESE & MUSHROOM FONDUE

**Makes 5 entrée servings**

## Ingredients:

½ cup dried mushrooms

1 cup boiling water

2 tablespoons unsalted butter

4 ounces fresh mixed mushrooms, sliced

1 small yellow onion, chopped

2 garlic cloves, smashed

1 teaspoon fresh thyme leaves

Kosher salt and fresh pepper to taste

$^1/_3$ cup dry white wine

½ cup half & half

8 ounces mozzarella cheese, cubed

1 ounce Parmesan cheese, cubed

8 ounces Swiss cheese, cubed

French bread

## Method:

1. *In a small bowl combine the dried mushrooms and water; set aside.*

2. *Melt the butter in a large sauté pan over medium-high heat.*

3. *When butter sizzles, add the mixed mushrooms, onions and garlic; spread them out and sauté until well browned.*

4. *Add the dried mushrooms and their soaking water to the pan to deglaze. Scrape up the brown bits from the bottom of the pan then transfer the pan contents to the blender.*

5. *Add remaining ingredients, except bread, to the blender; cover with lid.*

6. *Blend on LOW first to avoid splashing then increase speed to HIGH and blend for 4 minutes or until mixture is hot and cheese is melted.*

7. *Pour into a fondue pot and serve with French bread for dipping.*

**TIP**

You can save ¼ of the mushrooms after browning them to stir into the finished sauce for added texture.

ENTREES

# PEPPERONI PIZZA FONDUE

**Makes 4 entrée servings**

## Ingredients:

⅓ cup chicken stock

1 can (14 ounces) stewed tomatoes

½ cup pepperoni slices

½ cup Parmesan cheese, cubed

2 cups fresh mozzarella cheese, cubed

¼ cup sun dried tomatoes in oil, drained

4 garlic cloves

1 small yellow onion, peeled and quartered

¼ red bell pepper

⅓ cup tomato paste

2 teaspoons Italian seasoning

2 tablespoons fresh basil, sliced

Italian bread, cubed

## Method:

1. *Place all ingredients, except basil and bread, into the blender; cover with lid.*
2. *Blend on LOW until pieces are small (use stir stick as needed).*
3. *Increase speed to HIGH and blend for 4 minutes or until very steamy and cheese has melted.*
4. *Transfer to a fondue pot, top with basil and serve hot with bread for dipping.*

**TIP**

You can swap out ingredients just the way you would if building your favorite pizza.

# EASY SLOW COOKED MARINATED RIBS

**Makes 6 servings**

## Ingredients:

### For the Marinade:

1 small white onion, quartered

¼ cup vegetable oil

2 tablespoons paprika

2 tablespoons apple cider vinegar

1½ tablespoons kosher salt

1 tablespoon granulated sugar

1 tablespoon brown sugar, packed

1 teaspoon freshly ground pepper

½ teaspoon cayenne pepper

5 pounds pork ribs

### For the Ribs:

5 pounds pork ribs

BBQ sauce, for serving (optional)

## Method:

1. *Place all marinade ingredients into the blender; cover with lid.*
2. *Blend on HIGH for 30 seconds or until a smooth paste forms (use stir stick as needed).*
3. *Place ribs on a large pan and coat thoroughly with marinade mixture.*
4. *Cover and refrigerate for a minimum of 6 hours.*
5. *Place ribs into a slow cooker and cook for 8 hours according to manufacturer's instructions.*
6. *Remove from slow cooker and serve as desired.*

## TIP
To make these ribs in the oven, cook at 300°F, covered for 4-5 hours or until tender.

# EASY BLENDER EGG FOO YONG

**Makes 4-6 servings**

## Ingredients:

### For the Egg Mixture:

6 garlic cloves

1 piece of ginger (2 inches long), peeled

½ bunch cilantro, chopped

½ teaspoon chili flakes

2 teaspoons kosher salt

2 teaspoons soy sauce

6 large eggs

¼ cup cornstarch

2 teaspoons sesame oil

### For the Vegetables and Meat:

½ head green cabbage, thinly sliced

1 yellow onion, julienned

1 bunch green onions, sliced

2 large carrots, julienned

4 cups fresh baby spinach

1 red bell pepper, julienned

1 cup leftover ham or chicken, diced

Canola oil

Cooked rice

Soy sauce

## Method:

1. *Place all egg mixture ingredients into the blender; cover with lid.*
2. *Blend on LOW for 10 seconds then increase speed to HIGH and blend for 30 seconds.*
3. *Transfer mixture to a large mixing bowl.*
4. *Fold in remaining ingredients except canola oil, rice and soy sauce.*
5. *Stir until well mixed and all of the vegetables are coated with egg mixture.*
6. *Preheat a large skillet or griddle to medium-high heat.*
7. *Lightly oil the skillet or griddle.*
8. *Spoon ½ cup per patty of the mixture onto the skillet or griddle; spoon as many as will fit in the skillet or on the griddle (make sure to include some of the egg mixture with the vegetables when spooning).*
9. *Cook each side for 2 minutes or until brown.*
10. *Remove and repeat with remaining mixture.*
11. *Serve with rice and soy sauce.*

# MAC & CHEESE

**Makes 6 servings**

## Ingredients:

10 ounces extra-sharp Cheddar cheese, cubed

⅔ cup mozzarella cheese, cubed

1½ cups whole milk

½ small white onion, cut into chunks

1 teaspoon kosher salt

¼ teaspoon freshly ground pepper

½ teaspoon dry mustard powder

¼ teaspoon garlic powder

⅔ pound elbow macaroni, cooked

¼ cup Parmesan cheese, grated

## Method:

1. *Place all ingredients, except macaroni and Parmesan cheese, into the blender; cover with lid.*
2. *Blend on LOW until pieces are small (use stir stick as needed).*
3. *Increase speed to HIGH and blend for 6 minutes or until steamy and very hot.*
4. *Place macaroni into a large bowl.*
5. *Pour cheese mixture over the macaroni; stir well.*
6. *Serve macaroni topped with Parmesan cheese.*

# BUTTERMILK
## PIE

**Makes one 9-inch pie**

SWEET TREATS

## Ingredients:

1 cup granulated sugar

$^2/_3$ cup light brown sugar, packed

½ cup unsalted butter, melted

1 teaspoon pure vanilla extract

2 teaspoons white vinegar

¼ cup buttermilk

$^2/_3$ cup heavy cream

8 large egg yolks

1 prepared 9-inch pie crust, unbaked

Powdered Sugar

## Method:

1. *Preheat oven to 325°F.*
2. *Place all ingredients, except pie crust and powdered sugar, into the blender; cover with lid.*
3. *PULSE until mixture is smooth and frothy.*
4. *Pour mixture into the prepared pie crust.*
5. *Bake for 15 minutes then lower the oven temperature to 300°F.*
6. *Bake for an additional 40 minutes or until set.*
7. *Serve at room temperature dusted with powdered sugar.*

# CHOCOLATE & BANANA
## BREAD PUDDING

**Makes 6 servings**

## Ingredients:

4 cups croissants, cut into cubes

1½ cups semi-sweet chocolate chips

3 ripe bananas, sliced

2 overripe bananas, peeled

3 cups heavy whipping cream

6 large eggs

1 cup light brown sugar, packed

¼ teaspoon kosher salt

1 tablespoon vanilla extract

1 tablespoon fresh lemon juice

## Method:

1. *Preheat oven to 350°F.*
2. *Apply nonstick spray to 6 individual casserole dishes or ramekins.*
3. *Divide the croissant, chocolate and banana slices between the dishes; set aside.*
4. *Place remaining ingredients into the blender; cover with lid.*
5. *Blend on MEDIUM for 20 seconds (use stir stick as needed).*
6. *Pour the mixture evenly over the ingredients in each casserole dish.*
7. *Bake for 25 minutes or until well browned and gently set off-center.*
8. *Garnish as desired and serve hot or warm.*

# SWEET RICOTTA
## PUFFS

**Makes 30 puffs**

## Ingredients:

### For the Puffs:
15 ounces whole milk ricotta cheese

½ cup sour cream

½ cup granulated sugar

5 large eggs

½ teaspoon kosher salt

1 tablespoon vanilla extract

1 teaspoon ground cinnamon

4 teaspoons baking powder

1½ cups unbleached all purpose flour

### For Frying and Rolling:
4 cups canola or peanut oil

½ cup unsalted butter, melted

1 tablespoon ground cinnamon

1 cup granulated sugar

## Method:

1. *Place all puffs ingredients in the order listed into the blender; cover with lid.*
2. *Blend on LOW until smooth (use stir stick as needed).*
3. *In a deep Dutch oven, heat oil for frying until it reaches 350°F on a thermometer.*
4. *Using a small ice cream scoop, drop the batter 5-10 scoops at a time into the hot oil.*
5. *Fry for 90 seconds on each side or until golden brown.*
6. *Remove and drain on absorbent paper then repeat with remaining batter.*
7. *Pour melted butter into a bowl.*
8. *Combine the cinnamon and sugar in a separate bowl.*
9. *Roll each cooked puff first in butter, allowing excess to drip off, then roll to cover in cinnamon sugar.*
10. *Serve warm.*

# EASIEST CHOCOLATE
## CAKE

**Makes 4-6 servings**

## Ingredients:

**For the Cake:**

1½ cups all purpose flour

¾ cup granulated sugar

3 tablespoons cocoa powder

1 teaspoon baking soda

½ teaspoon kosher salt

1 teaspoon pure vanilla extract

¼ cup vegetable oil

1 cup water

1 tablespoon white vinegar

**For the Glaze:**

¾ cup granulated sugar

¼ cup water

2 tablespoons cocoa powder

1 tablespoon vegetable oil

1 teaspoon pure vanilla extract

Pinch of kosher salt

## Method:

1. *Preheat the oven to 350°F.*
2. *Butter an 8x8-inch baking dish; set aside.*
3. *Place all cake ingredients into the blender; cover with lid.*
4. *Blend on HIGH for 30 seconds then pour the batter into the prepared baking dish.*
5. *Bake for 25 minutes or until a toothpick inserted off-center comes out clean.*
6. *Rinse the blender then add all glaze ingredients; cover with lid.*
7. *Blend on HIGH for 3 minutes or until glaze is very steamy and hot.*
8. *Pour hot glaze over the baked cake and spread it to the edges using a spatula.*
9. *Serve cake warm.*

**TIP**

If you want a thicker glaze, let it cool first before spreading it on the cake.

# EASIEST CHOCOLATE CAKE

**Makes 4-6 servings**

## Ingredients:

**For the Cake:**

1½ cups all purpose flour

¾ cup granulated sugar

3 tablespoons cocoa powder

1 teaspoon baking soda

½ teaspoon kosher salt

1 teaspoon pure vanilla extract

¼ cup vegetable oil

1 cup water

1 tablespoon white vinegar

**For the Glaze:**

¾ cup granulated sugar

¼ cup water

2 tablespoons cocoa powder

1 tablespoon vegetable oil

1 teaspoon pure vanilla extract

Pinch of kosher salt

## Method:

1. *Preheat the oven to 350°F.*
2. *Butter an 8x8-inch baking dish; set aside.*
3. *Place all cake ingredients into the blender; cover with lid.*
4. *Blend on HIGH for 30 seconds then pour the batter into the prepared baking dish.*
5. *Bake for 25 minutes or until a toothpick inserted off-center comes out clean.*
6. *Rinse the blender then add all glaze ingredients; cover with lid.*
7. *Blend on HIGH for 3 minutes or until glaze is very steamy and hot.*
8. *Pour hot glaze over the baked cake and spread it to the edges using a spatula.*
9. *Serve cake warm.*

**TIP**

If you want a thicker glaze, let it cool first before spreading it on the cake.

# GRAPEFRUIT
## TARTS

**Makes 4-6 servings**

## Ingredients:

¼ cup sour cream

3 large egg yolks

1 can (14 ounces) sweetened condensed milk

1 tablespoon Ruby Red grapefruit zest

⅓ cup fresh Ruby Red grapefruit juice

6 tart shells, lined with desired crust

Whipped cream or meringue

## Method:

1. *Preheat oven to 300°F.*
2. *Place the sour cream, yolks, condensed milk, zest and juice into the blender.*
3. *Cover with lid.*
4. *Blend on LOW for 30 seconds or until no visible zest pieces remain.*
5. *Divide mixture between the tart shells.*
6. *Place tart shells on a cookie sheet and bake in the oven for 25 minutes (filling should still be a bit jiggly when done).*
7. *Remove tarts and let cool completely then chill for 2 hours or until cold.*
8. *Top with whipped cream or meringue and serve.*

## TIP
You can turn these into lemon or lime tarts by substituting the zest and the juice that you like.

# GRASSHOPPER
## TARTS

**Makes 6 tarts**

## Ingredients:

### For the Crust:
30 chocolate wafers
6 tablespoons unsalted butter, melted

### For the Grasshopper Filling:
1½ cups heavy cream
½ teaspoon vanilla extract
3 tablespoons powdered sugar
¼ cup crème de menthe liqueur
½ teaspoon peppermint extract
⅓ cup white chocolate chips, melted

## Method:

1. Place wafers into the blender; cover with lid.
2. PULSE until fine crumbs are achieved.
3. Transfer crumbs to a mixing bowl.
4. Pour the butter over the crumbs; stir to combine.
5. Divide the crumbs between 6 small tart pans and press the crumbs into the bottom and sides of each pan to make a crust; set aside.
6. Rinse the blender then add the cream, vanilla and sugar; cover with lid.
7. PULSE until cream thickens without becoming too stiff.
8. Transfer cream mixture to a mixing bowl.
9. Fold in remaining ingredients; stir until smooth.
10. Divide the mixture between the crumb-lined tart pans.
11. Chill for 30 minutes then garnish as desired and serve cold.

# MANGO & LIME
# SEMIFREDDO

**Makes 4 cups**

## Ingredients:

½ cup granulated sugar

¼ cup water

2 cups fresh mango, peeled and chopped

½ cup fresh lime juice

1 teaspoon lime zest, grated

1 cup heavy cream

## Method:

1. *Pour sugar and water into a small saucepan over medium-high heat.*

2. *Bring to a boil and stir until sugar is melted then set aside.*

3. *Place the mango into the blender; cover with lid.*

4. *Blend on HIGH until pureed.*

5. *Add the lime juice, zest and sugar mixture; blend on HIGH until combined.*

6. *Pour mixture into a baking pan; freeze for 1 hour or until almost frozen.*

7. *Clean blender then pour in the heavy cream.*

8. *Blend on LOW until soft peaks form.*

9. *Using a knife, break up the frozen mango mixture and add to the blender.*

10. *Blend on LOW until smooth and well combined with the heavy cream (use stir stick as needed).*

11. *Line a 9x5-inch loaf pan with plastic wrap and pour mixture into the pan.*

12. *Fold plastic wrap over the top and freeze for 4 hours.*

13. *Use plastic wrap to lift semifreddo from the pan and place on a cutting board; cut into 1-inch slices and serve.*

## TIP

If you want to make a colorful contrast, divide the mixture in half and color one half green using a few drops of food coloring then layer into the pan before freezing.

SWEET TREATS

# HOMEMADE
## SNO CONES

**Makes 4 servings**

## Ingredients:

### For the Sno Cones:
4 cups ice
8 tablespoons flavored syrup

### Strawberry Syrup:
1½ cups fresh strawberries
⅓ cup water
⅔ cup granulated sugar
2 tablespoons lemon juice

### Kiwi Syrup:
5 ripe kiwis, peeled
¼ cup water
⅔ cup granulated sugar

### Blueberry Syrup:
1½ cups fresh blueberries
⅓ cup water
⅔ cup granulated sugar
2 tablespoons lemon juice

### Pineapple Syrup:
1½ cups fresh pineapple chunks
⅓ cup water
⅔ cup granulated sugar
1-2 drops yellow food coloring

## Method:

1. *Place the ice into the blender; cover with lid.*
2. *Blend on HIGH until ice is fine like snow.*
3. *Scoop crushed ice into small cups or cones.*
4. *Place desired syrup ingredients into the blender; cover with lid.*
5. *Blend on HIGH until smooth.*
6. *Top cones with 2 tablespoons of syrup and serve.*
7. *Syrup can be stored refrigerated for up to 1 week or frozen for up to 3 months.*

## TIP
The easiest way to dispense the syrup is to use an inexpensive squeeze bottle.

# WOLF'S FAVORITE
## MANGO SORBET

**Makes 1 quart**

## Ingredients:

4 cups frozen mango chunks

½ cup granulated sugar or sugar substitute

Juice and zest from 1 lime (optional)

2 cups mango juice

## Method:

1. *Place all ingredients, except mango juice, into the blender; cover with lid.*

2. *Blend on LOW until only small pieces remain (use stir stick as needed).*

3. *Increase speed to HIGH.*

4. *While blending, slowly pour the mango juice through the filler cap hole until thick and smooth (do not over-blend or it will melt quickly).*

5. *Remove and serve.*

## TIP
You can use this recipe as a template to make other sorbets. Just use similar frozen fruits and juice.

# BLUEBERRY
# VANILLA SORBET

**Makes 4 servings**

## Ingredients:

1 vanilla bean, split lengthwise

1 cup water

1/3 cup granulated sugar

4 cups fresh or frozen blueberries

4 teaspoons fresh lemon juice

## Method:

1. *Scrape seeds from vanilla bean then place the seeds and pod into a small saucepan.*
2. *Add water and sugar to the saucepan; bring to a boil over medium-high heat.*
3. *Reduce heat to low and let simmer for 10 minutes or until mixture is reduced to about 1/3 cup.*
4. *Discard vanilla pods then pour the mixture into the blender.*
5. *Add remaining ingredients to the blender; cover with lid.*
6. *Blend on HIGH until pureed.*
7. *Pour mixture into a shallow metal pan; cover with plastic wrap.*
8. *Freeze for a minimum of 4 hours.*
9. *Using a fork, scrape the top of the frozen mixture to create loose crystals.*
10. *Place the crystals into serving bowls and freeze for 30 minutes before serving.*

# GRAPEFRUIT
# SORBET

**Makes 4 cups**

## Ingredients:

10 Ruby Red grapefruits, washed

⅔ cup granulated sugar

A few drops of red food coloring (optional)

## Method:

1. *Zest 5 of the grapefruits.*

2. *Juice all of the grapefruits.*

3. *Strain the juice to remove any seeds.*

4. *Place the zest, juice and sugar into the blender; cover with lid.*

5. *Blend on HIGH for 30 seconds or until no pieces of zest remain.*

6. *Taste carefully and adjust sweetness if needed.*

7. *Add coloring if desired.*

8. *Chill mixture until very cold.*

9. *Cover and freeze sorbet in a container, or if you have an ice cream machine, use to spin according to manufacturer's directions.*

10. *When frozen, chop up into chunks and PULSE in the blender until smooth.*

11. *Sorbet will keep covered and frozen for up to 3 days.*

# ORANGE CREAMSICLE POPS

**Makes 6 pops**

## Ingredients:

⅓ cup whole milk

4 scoops vanilla ice cream

Zest from 1 orange

1 cup fresh orange juice

1 teaspoon vanilla extract

¼ teaspoon Fiori Di Sicilia (optional), see source page 140

1-2 drops orange food coloring (optional)

## Method:

1. *Place all ingredients into the blender; cover with lid.*
2. *Blend on HIGH until creamy and smooth (use stir stick as needed).*
3. *Pour mixture into 6 small paper cups or popsicle molds.*
4. *Freeze for 1 hour or until fairly firm.*
5. *Insert wooden sticks into the center of each pop and serve.*

# CHOCOLATE
# ICE CREAM

**Makes 4 servings**

## Ingredients:

1 cup half & half

⅓ cup granulated sugar

⅓ cup powdered milk

½ cup chocolate fudge sundae topping

1 teaspoon vanilla extract

1 teaspoon instant espresso powder

4 cups ice cubes

## Method:

1. *Place all ingredients into the blender; cover with lid.*
2. *Blend on LOW for 30 seconds (use stir stick as needed).*
3. *Blend on HIGH for an additional 1 minute or until smooth.*
4. *Scoop into pretty serving dishes and garnish as desired.*
5. *Serve immediately.*

## TIP
You can make this into butterscotch ice cream by using butterscotch topping and omitting the espresso powder.

# POPEYE'S
# ICE CREAM

**Makes 4 cups**

## Ingredients:

2 cups spinach, lightly packed

⅔ cup powdered milk

¾ cup coconut milk

¼ cup cream of coconut

½ teaspoon vanilla extract

2 cups ice cubes

## Method:

1. *Place all ingredients into the blender; cover with lid.*

2. *Blend on HIGH for 30 seconds or until smooth (use stir stick as needed).*

3. *Serve immediately or place into a freezer-safe container.*

4. *Ice cream will keep in the freezer for up to 1 week.*

## TIP
Dont worry, you will not be able to taste the spinach in this recipe.

# INSTANT
# PUMPKIN MOUSSE

**Makes 6 servings**

## Ingredients:

2 cups heavy cream

1 can (15 ounces) solid pack pumpkin

²/₃ cup brown sugar, packed

2 teaspoons molasses

2 teaspoons ground cinnamon

1 teaspoon ground ginger

½ teaspoon ground nutmeg

¼ teaspoon ground cloves

¼ teaspoon ground allspice

Pinch of kosher salt

2 teaspoons fresh lemon juice

1 teaspoon vanilla extract

## Method:

1. *Pour heavy cream into the blender; cover with lid.*
2. *PULSE until cream has thickened (do not over mix); set aside.*
3. *In a bowl, combine remaining ingredients; beat using a hand whisk until smooth.*
4. *Using a spatula, scrape the cream on top of the pumpkin mixture.*
5. *Gently fold the two together until the color is uniform; do not over mix.*
6. *Spoon into cups and serve.*

# QUICK STRAWBERRY
# MOUSSE

**Makes 4 servings**

SWEET TREATS

## Ingredients:

½ cup fresh strawberries

½ cup powdered sugar

1½ cups heavy cream

Strawberry puree and strawberries, for topping

## Method:

1. *Place strawberries, powdered sugar and cream into the blender; cover with lid.*
2. *Blend on LOW until cream thickens (use stir stick as needed).*
3. *Layer into serving glasses with strawberry puree and fresh strawberries.*
4. *Serve cold.*

## TIP
Make this recipe your own by substituting your favorite berries.

# BERRY & RHUBARB GELATIN

**Makes 4 servings**

## Ingredients:

2 teaspoons orange zest

2 cups rhubarb, fresh or frozen, chopped

2 cup fresh strawberries, sliced

1 cup dry white wine

$\frac{2}{3}$ cup water

$\frac{1}{2}$ cup granulated sugar

2 tablespoons powdered unflavored gelatin

3 tablespoons cold water

## Method:

1. *Place zest, rhubarb, strawberries, wine, water and sugar into a large saucepan over medium-high heat; bring to a boil.*

2. *Reduce heat to low and simmer, uncovered, for 10 minutes or until rhubarb is broken up; set aside.*

3. *In a small saucepan, sprinkle the gelatin over cold water and let stand for 5 minutes.*

4. *Heat the gelatin mixture over low heat for 2-3 minutes or until gelatin has melted and is clear; set aside.*

5. *Place the rhubarb mixture into the blender; cover with lid.*

6. *Blend on HIGH for 20 seconds or until pureed (use stir stick as needed).*

7. *In a bowl, combine the rhubarb mixture with the gelatin mixture; mix well.*

8. *Divide among 4 wine goblets and loosely cover with plastic wrap.*

9. *Refrigerate for 6 hours or until set before serving.*

# APPLE
# BUTTER

**Makes 4 servings**

## Ingredients:

2 pounds Fuji apples, cored and quartered

1 cup water

⅓ cup cider vinegar

1 cup granulated sugar

2 tablespoons fresh lemon juice

2 teaspoons lemon zest, grated

1 teaspoon ground cinnamon

¼ teaspoon kosher salt

SWEET TREATS

## Method:

1. *Place apples, water and vinegar into a large saucepan over medium-high heat; bring to a boil.*

2. *Cover then reduce heat to low; let simmer for 20 minutes or until apples are very soft.*

3. *Remove from heat and let cool for 5 minutes.*

4. *Place apple mixture into the blender; cover with lid.*

5. *Blend on HIGH for 30 seconds or until pureed (use stir stick as needed).*

6. *Transfer apple mixture to a large saucepan over medium heat; add the sugar and stir to dissolve the sugar.*

7. *Add remaining ingredients to the saucepan; stir to combine.*

8. *Reduce heat to low and simmer for 45 minutes or until mixture is very thick and smooth.*

9. *Allow to completely cool then pour into sealable jars.*

10. *Apple butter will keep in the refrigerator for 2 weeks or in the freezer for 2 months.*

# VANILLA PANNA COTTA

**Makes 4 servings**

## Ingredients:

½ vanilla bean, split in half lengthwise

1½ cups heavy cream

½ cup whole milk

1½ teaspoons unflavored, powdered gelatin

2 tablespoons water

⅓ cup sugar

A small pinch of kosher salt

## Method:

1. *Place the vanilla bean, cream and milk into a microwave-safe bowl.*
2. *Microwave until very hot.*
3. *Let rest for 10 minutes, stirring occasionally to steep flavor from the vanilla bean.*
4. *In a small cup, mix together the gelatin and water until blended.*
5. *Let gelatin mixture rest for 5 minutes.*
6. *Microwave gelatin mixture for 10 seconds or until hot and the gelatin has melted.*
7. *Pour the vanilla mixture, gelatin mixture and remaining ingredients into the blender; cover with lid.*
8. *Blend on HIGH for 30 seconds or until foamy.*
9. *Strain mixture through a fine strainer to remove the vanilla bean pod pieces.*
10. *Pour into four 4-ounce ramekins, champagne flutes or small bowls.*
11. *Chill for 3 hours or until set.*
12. *Serve cold.*

# ENTIRE LEMON
# LEMONADE

**Makes 1 quart**

## Ingredients:

4 bright skinned lemons, scrubbed and halved

½ to ⅔ cup granulated sugar or sugar substitute

3 cups ice cubes

3 cups club soda or lemon lime soda

## Method:

1. *Place all ingredients into the blender; cover with lid.*

2. *Blend on HIGH until no lemon chunks remain (use stir stick as needed).*

3. *Either serve as is or strain to remove pulp.*

4. *Add additional ice cubes and club soda if desired.*

5. *Serve immediately.*

**TIP**

If you are going to store any leftover lemonade, strain first or it will turn bitter.

# ROOT JUICE

**Makes 1 serving**

## Ingredients:

1 small beet, peeled and cubed
1 small carrot, cubed
1 ginger root slice
1 tablespoon sugar
Zest and juice of 1 lemon
1 cup carrot juice
½ cup ice cubes

## Method:

1. *Place all ingredients into the blender; cover with lid.*
2. *Blend on HIGH for 1 minute or until smooth (use stir stick as needed).*
3. *Strain if desired and serve immediately.*

**TIP**

Freeze extras in an ice cube tray
then add a cube to lemon-lime
soda for a lovely color and taste.

# MEXICAN
# HOT CHOCOLATE

**Makes 2 servings**

## Ingredients:

2 cups whole milk

2 ounces semi-sweet chocolate chips

4 teaspoons granulated sugar

½ teaspoon vanilla extract

¼ teaspoon ground cinnamon

## Method:

1. *Place all ingredients into a small saucepan over medium-low heat.*
2. *Simmer for 2-3 minutes or until chocolate is melted.*
3. *Pour mixture into the blender; cover with lid.*
4. *Blend on HIGH for 15 seconds or until smooth and frothy.*
5. *Pour into mugs and serve.*

**TIP**

If you can find it, use real Mexican chocolate. It is sold in round discs and contains cinnamon.

# LYCHEE & RASPBERRY FIZZ

**Makes 1 serving**

## Ingredients:

1½ cups canned or fresh lychees

½ cup fresh raspberries

1 tablespoon granulated sugar

¼ cup ice cubes

½ cup cold ginger ale

## Method:

1. *Place all ingredients, except ginger ale, into the blender; cover with lid.*
2. *Blend on HIGH for 30 seconds or until smooth (use stir stick as needed).*
3. *Fill a glass 1/3 with lychee mixture then top off with ginger ale until full.*
4. *Serve immediately.*

**TIP**
If you don't like lychee, you can substitute it with banana.

# ICED COFFEE FRAPPE

**Makes 2 servings**

## Ingredients:

1⅓ cups strong brewed coffee

½ cup half & half

2 tablespoons granulated sugar

## Method:

1. *Pour coffee into an ice cube tray and freeze for a minimum of 4 hours.*
2. *Place coffee cubes and remaining ingredients into the blender; cover with lid.*
3. *Blend on HIGH for 15 seconds or until smooth (use stir stick as needed).*
4. *Pour into chilled glasses and serve.*

**TIP**
Leftover morning coffee is perfect for this recipe.

# MELON & KIWI SMOOTHIE

**Makes 1 serving**

## Ingredients:

½ cup honeydew melon chunks

2 kiwis, peeled

2 teaspoons honey

½ cup Greek yogurt

½ cup whole milk

½ cup ice cubes

## Method:

1. *Place all ingredients into the blender; cover with lid.*
2. *Blend on HIGH for 30 seconds or until smooth (use stir stick as needed).*
3. *Serve immediately.*

**TIP**

For a great protein-packed smoothie, add a scoop of protein powder.

# STRAWBERRY & APRICOT
# SMOOTHIE

**Makes 1 serving**

## Ingredients:

2 apricots, halved and pitted

8 large strawberries, hulled

2 teaspoons honey

½ cup Greek yogurt

¼ cup whole milk

½ cup ice cubes

## Method:

1. *Place all ingredients into the blender; cover with lid.*
2. *Blend on HIGH for 30 seconds (use stir stick as needed).*
3. *Serve immediately.*

## TIP

Buy the most fragrant apricots you can find. If they don't have a fruity smell, they will most likely not pack alot of flavor.

# MANGO, COCONUT & LIME SMOOTHIE

**Makes 1 serving**

## Ingredients:

Zest and juice of 1 lime
1/3 cup cream of coconut
1 ripe mango, peeled and chunked
1 cup ice cubes

## Method:

1. *Place all ingredients into the blender; cover with lid.*
2. *Blend on HIGH for 30 seconds or until smooth (use stir stick as needed).*
3. *Serve immediately.*

## TIP

Don't confuse cream of coconut with coconut milk.
Cream of coconut is sweetened and has intense
coconut flavor. Coconut milk is thin and unsweetened.

# CHOCOLATE
# CHIP MILKSHAKE

**Makes 2 servings**

## Ingredients:

4 scoops vanilla ice cream

½ cup whole milk

½ teaspoon vanilla extract

¼ cup milk chocolate chips

2 tablespoons chocolate syrup, divided

## Method:

1. *Place the ice cream, milk and vanilla into the blender; cover with lid.*

2. *Blend on HIGH for 20 seconds or until smooth (add more milk if desired).*

3. *Pour the chocolate chips through the filler cap hole and PULSE until chips are chopped into small pieces.*

4. *To serve, pour 1 tablespoon chocolate syrup in the bottom of each glass then pour the shake to the top.*

## TIP

For a treat, top with a generous amount of whipped cream and a maraschino cherry.

# MELON BERRY SHAKE

**Makes 1 serving**

## Ingredients:

½ cup watermelon chunks, peeled

1 cup fresh strawberries, hulled

1 cup vanilla ice cream

2 tablespoons whole milk

## Method:

1. *Place all ingredients into the blender; cover with lid.*

2. *Blend on HIGH for 30 seconds or until smooth (use stir stick as needed).*

3. *Serve immediately.*

# BUTTER PECAN
# MILKSHAKE

**Makes 2 servings**

## Ingredients:

4 scoops vanilla ice cream

¼ teaspoon vanilla extract

¼ teaspoon maple extract

⅛ teaspoon butter vanilla extract

½ cup whole milk

½ cup pecans, toasted, chopped and divided

Whipped cream

## Method:

1. *Place all ingredients, except pecans and whipped cream, into the blender; cover with lid.*

2. *Blend on HIGH for 20 seconds or until smooth (use stir stick as needed); add more milk if desired.*

3. *Pour ¼ cup pecans through the filler cap hole; PULSE until pecans are chopped into small pieces.*

4. *Place 1 tablespoon of the remaining pecans into the bottom of each glass.*

5. *Pour shake into the glasses.*

6. *Top with whipped cream, sprinkle with pecans and serve.*

## TIP
The amazing flavor in this recipe comes from the toasted pecans. To toast, spread pecans on a cookie sheet and place in the oven at 350°F for 15 minutes.

# SOURCE PAGE

Here are some of my favorite places to find ingredients that are not readily available at grocery stores as well as kitchen tools and supplies that help you become a better cook.

## Chocosphere

P.O. Box 2237
Tualatin, OR 97062
877-992-4623

Excellent quality cocoa (Callebaut)
All Chocolates
Jimmies and sprinkles
**www.chocosphere.com**

## Gluten Free Mall

4927 Sonoma HWY Suite C1
Santa Rosa, CA 95409
707-509-4528

All ingredients needed for gluten-free baking
**www.glutenfreemall.com**

## D & G Occasions

625 Herndon Ave.
Orlando, FL 32803
407-894-4458

My favorite butter vanilla extract by Magic Line, cake and candy making supplies, citric acid, pure fruit oils, professional food colorings, ultra thin flexible spatulas, large selection of sprinkles and jimmies, unusual birthday candles, pure vanilla extract, pastry bags and tips, parchment, off-set spatulas, oven and candy thermometers, kitchen timers
**www.dandgoccasions.com**

## The Bakers Catalogue at King Arthur Flour

135 Route 5 South
P.O. Box 1010
Norwich, VT 05055

Pure fruit oils, citric acid, silicone spatulas, digital timers, oven thermometers, real truffle oil, off-set spatulas, measuring cups and spoons, knives, ice cream scoops, cheesecloth, microplane graters, cookie sheets, baking pans
**www.kingarthurflour.com**

# Penzeys Spices

P.O. Box 924
Brookfield, WI 53045
800-741-7787

Spices, extracts, seasonings and more
**www.penzeys.com**

# Fortune Products, Inc.

205 Hickory Creek Road
Marble Falls, TX 78654
830-693-6111

Inexpensive, hand-held Accusharp knife sharpeners
**www.accusharp.com**

# Vanilla From Tahiti

Nui Enterprises
501 Chapala St. Suite A
Santa Barbara, CA 93101
805-965-5153
**www.vanillafromtahiti.com**

# Rolling Pin Kitchen Emporium

P.O. Box 21798
Long Beach, CA 90801
949-221-9399

Cheesecloth, inexpensive "harp" shaped vegetable peelers, measuring cups and spoons, knives, vast array of kitchen tools including microplane graters, blow torches, baking pans and dishes
**www.rollingpin.com**

# Whole Foods

550 Bowie St.
Austin, TX 78703
512-477-4455

Grains, citric acid, natural and organic products, xanthan gum, gluten-free baking items, real truffle oil
**www.wholefoods.com**

**For more of Marian's delicious ideas, please visit:**

**www.mariangetz.com**

**INDEX**